INSPIRATIONAL HOCKEY STORIES FOR YOUNG READERS

12 UNBELIEVABLE TRUE TALES TO INSPIRE AND AMAZE YOUNG HOCKEY LOVERSS

Mike Johnson

CONTENTS

ATTENTION:

DO YOU WANT MY FUTURE BOOKS AT HEAVY DISCOUNTS AND EVEN FOR FREE?

**HEAD OVER TO \underline{\text{WWW.SECRETREADS.COM}}
AND JOIN MY SECRET BOOK CLUB!**

INTRODUCTION

Ice hockey is a sport that combines multiple skills in a way that few other sports come close to emulating. It requires agility, power, finesse, and mental sharpness. It also involves quick thinking and core body strength. The unique set of talents needed to be successful on the ice creates magical moments that bring fans to their feet because they understand what it takes. Those same fans love the players on their favorite team, the ones who electrify the crowd with excitement whenever they take the ice. Fans may buy a jersey with their favorite player's name and number, emulate how that player moves on the ice, or even ask for an autograph. They long to learn more about their favorite players and understand how that player came to be so special.

Even more special, though, is the human element behind the sport of hockey. Every game, 18 players on each team put their bodies on the line for each other, for the emblem on the jersey, and for the fans who support them. When a team of individuals comes together, stories naturally emerge. Some of those stories can captivate an audience. Some of those become revered, and a select few become legendary. Fans of the game learn these stories, drawing inspiration from the grit, tenacity, and relentlessness that these individuals demonstrate. Hockey players simply don't quit, even against the advice of medical professionals.

In this book, we're going to look at some of the most inspiring, motivating stories to emerge from the world of ice hockey. We'll look at individuals and teams that overcame the odds and pushed forward. Whether it was a player fighting through injury or illness, a team recovering from a terrible loss that wasn't on the scoreboard, or families fighting more than one battle at a time, this book will show that hockey players are just as tough mentally as they are physically. Some of these stories had lasting impacts, changing the game forever.

We'll look at how the NHL created an All-Star Game to help an injured player.

We'll see how a player who was blind in one eye developed the first visor, helping all visually impaired players participate in the game he loves.

We'll find out how a young man who was paralyzed while playing the game never gave up the fight to help as many people as he could with his talents.

We'll try to figure out how one of the greatest to ever play the game was able to come back from a dangerous cancer battle.

We'll take a deep dive into one of the most iconic moments in Stanley Cup Finals history involving a big hit, a concussion, and a bigger goal.

We'll look closely at the only player to play at the professional level across six decades.

We'll see what happens when a talented player suffers through numerous injuries and illnesses but won't quit.

We'll watch a championship team deal with tragedy in the offseason and see how they respond in the following year.

We'll see how one man broke the NHL's color barrier, and what he did for the sport after his career came to an end.

We'll feel the pain of an NHL goaltender as his wife is diagnosed with cancer, and we'll wonder if he can continue to perform with that stress on his mind.

We'll learn the story of the only NHL player to be legally deaf, and we'll catch up on how he has helped the game.

Finally, we'll try to figure out how one player scored an overtime goal on a broken leg, and then played in the next game for the Stanley Cup!

Whether you're new to the game or a grizzled veteran, the stories in these pages are for you. We hope that you'll find inspiration from these stories, and perhaps a player's strength in difficult times will help you persevere when times are tough at your end of the rink.

Let's drop the puck.

STORY 1:

GREG NEELD'S VISOR

In today's hockey world, visors are required pieces of equipment to protect the eyes of the player. Of course, throughout the history of the game, there were periods when no one wore visors - or even helmets at all. But, after the introduction of the helmet back in 1927, several decades passed before the visor made an appearance on the ice. Unsurprisingly, it took a severe injury before one player decided to invent and then wear that helpful piece of equipment that is now a staple of the game around the world.

Greg Neeld, who is now in his late 60s working as a successful businessman, once had a dream of playing professional hockey. Like most Canadian youngsters with similar hopes, he attempted to work his way up through the junior leagues, which are designed for younger players. These leagues also attract the attention of pro league scouts, hence their popularity for players who do not take the collegiate route.

Neeld was performing well during the 1973-74 season in the Ontario Hockey Association, but on December 7, 1973, when his Toronto Marlboros faced the Kitchener Rangers, Neeld suffered a dangerous injury.

As Neeld went to retrieve the puck in his own zone, a routine play for every defenseman who has ever played the game, he attempted to lean down low to escape from the forecheck of Rangers' Dave Maloney. Sometimes, opposing players will rush into the zone and attempt to check the defenseman off the puck. Neeld was leaning down in an attempt to avoid this contact. However, Maloney tried to hook Neeld with his stick to prevent him from skating away from the pressure. Hooking was not called as a penalty as often back then, because it was seen as a way to keep players from moving too fast and causing injury. Because Neeld was bent down low, Maloney's stick struck Neeld in the face. Neeld fell to the ice, his hands over his face as he screamed in pain.

As Neeld gripped his face and left the ice, unable to see, dread undoubtedly set into every player's chest. It's a feeling that comes whenever an injury takes place. It's a reminder that everyone on the ice is a human being; that there are no enemies in life.

When all was said and done that day, the resulting injury caused Neeld to lose his left eye. Maloney was assessed a five-minute major on the play.

For most hockey players, this would be the end of the story. The player would resign from their team and move into another field of work. But Neeld dug deep for a way to keep his dream alive. He would not be denied in his bid to play hockey professionally.

While his 1973-74 season was cut short, he joined a new team for the next season, the Calgary Centennials. To play on this new team, though, Neeld would need a way to protect his good eye. The traditional cage worn over the face, typically for children, obstructed Neeld's vision and would not work for the high level of play of the OHL. Neeld turned to his father for help, and together, they developed the first visor in hockey.

Some players likely judged Neeld for wearing face protection. It was for kids. That's what players used to think, up until the mid-2010s, even in the NHL. But Neeld ignored the stubbornness of the players around him who thought the visor was a sign of weakness.

With that visor on his helmet for every one of the 62 games he played in that season, Neeld posted a whopping 29 goals and 30 assists, along with 186 penalty minutes. To be almost a point-per-game defenseman with one eye is truly a feat. And guess what? Professional scouts took notice. His dream was trending in the right direction.

Neeld spent part of the 1974-75 season with the Buffalo Norsemen, a team competing in the inaugural season of the North American Hockey League. It was his last year with a junior team because, during the summer of 1975, he was eligible to be drafted by professional teams. There were whispers that he might be selected, but teams were also aware of his condition. Whether or not he would be able to make it into the league from a legal standpoint was still something that had to be figured out.

Two teams from two different leagues drafted Neeld, a testament to his abilities. In the World Hockey Association, Neeld was drafted 40th overall by the Minnesota Fighting Saints. Needless to say, for Neeld to have made it this far with only one functional eye, was spectacular. The impressive record didn't stop there, though. The second team to draft him was the Buffalo Sabres of the National Hockey League, who selected Neeld in the fourth round with the 71st overall pick.

For the moment, it seemed as though Neeld had made his dream come true. An NHL team had selected him to be part of their organization! However, the NHL rules had something to say about his participation in the league. As with any business, there are rules which help the NHL avoid unnecessary risk. An unnecessary risk in this situation, according to the NHL, would be to allow a player with only one eye to play on the ice with the strongest, fastest players in the world.

Neeld did not doubt that he could compete at the highest level. But he had to appeal his case to the league for permission to enter. Equipped with his visor-laden helmet, Neeld spoke to the league's governing body in hopes to convince them that his helmet would adequately protect his good eye. However, his appeal was unsuccessful. Greg Neeld was prohibited from playing hockey in the NHL after the governors voted against a rule change to accommodate Neeld's request.

Again, this would be the end of most hockey players' hopes and dreams. The story would end here, and the injured individual would find another place to put their effort. Greg Neeld, though, would not be deterred. Although his path to the NHL was closed, there was another professional league in North America to accommodate him: The International Hockey League.

After a couple more years playing junior hockey with the Toronto Toros of the WHA and Erie Blades of the NAHL, which included a campaign of 64 points in 73 games with Erie, Neeld made his way to the Dayton/Grand Rapids Owls of the IHL. While Neeld did not play any full seasons in the league, he posted impressive numbers in the 1978-79 season, when he played seven games with the Kalamazoo Wings, 21 games with the Toledo Golddiggers, and 42 games with the Muskegon Mohawks. Over those 70 games, Neeld posted 10 goals and 38 assists, along with 284 penalty minutes.

At that time, Neeld was forced to end his hockey career. But, again, that is not the end of his story. Some players, when they hang up the skates, go home to live a quiet life with their families and friends, enjoying the rest that they have earned through their battles on the ice. And there is nothing wrong with that. But Neeld's impact on the game, and all of those who will go on to play it in the future, was strong.

In the decades that have followed, eye injuries have decreased significantly because of rules that were put into place because of Neeld's story. Players were required to wear visors through the Junior A level beginning in the

1980s, and in 2013, the NHL began requiring visors for all incoming players. The game itself, at every level of competition in the world, was impacted by Greg Neeld and his dream.

Greg Neeld never laced up the skates and donned the jersey of an NHL team, so some doubters may say that he failed in his dream. Others can understand the impact that he had on the game because of his tenacity and refusal to quit. If he had turned away from the game when his injury took place, who knows how long it would have taken the world of hockey to turn their attention to the dangers of injuries to the face. Thankfully, because of Greg Neeld, we don't have to wonder about that future. Instead, we get to enjoy a game where the players are better protected, and that is an impact worth celebrating.

So, the next time you're faced with an obstacle that seems impassable, remember Greg Neeld and his dream. More importantly, though, remember that your dream may not come true, but if you keep fighting and pushing forward, you might just make the world around you a better place in the process. And, who knows, perhaps your desire to succeed will give those around you the motivation and inspiration to do the same.

STORY 2:

TRAVIS ROY'S LEGACY

In the United States, the path to professional hockey does not always go through the junior leagues as it often does in Canada. Many young American players will take the path through collegiate hockey, where they can wear the sweater of their university while they study to earn a degree. College hockey in the United States is quite popular, and many teams around the country have cemented themselves as stalwarts of the sport. The NCAA (National Collegiate Athletic Association) even has an annual tournament for the best teams across the country. They call it the Frozen Four, a comparison to the basketball tournament's Final Four.

One of the storied hockey schools is Boston University, and one of its best-known players was Travis Roy.

Travis had hockey on his mind from a very young age, and he took proactive steps on his path to Boston University. Among the school's attractive accolades at the time were four national championships, including the 1995 title. Any young player would love the opportunity to join a great team, and it would be even more exciting to make the roster of the defending national champions. It helped that Travis Roy lived in that region of the country, so attending a nearby school would be a natural goal.

While in high school, Travis attended three different high schools (Yarmouth High, North Yarmouth Academy, and Tabor Academy) as he made a name for himself in the hockey circles. Those moves coupled with successful campaigns on the ice earned Travis a scholarship to play hockey at his dream school, Boston University, where he would study communications.

In the fall of 1995, Travis played his first game, at 20 years of age, for Boston University. It was October 20, to be exact. Travis took to the ice on his first shift, and 11 seconds into that first-ever shift for Travis Roy, tragedy struck.

Travis attempted to check opposing player Mitch Vig of the University of North Dakota, but Travis lost his balance during the contact. Unable to regain his balance in time, Travis collided with the boards at an awkward angle. He fell to the ice, unmoving. Coaches and trainers rushed to his aid. The arena was silent as they worked to determine his injury. Just 11 seconds on the ice, 11 seconds wearing the Boston University jersey, and it had all come to a halt. A dream was ripped away.

The impact against the boards broke the fourth and fifth cervical vertebrae of Travis' neck, leaving him instantly paralyzed from the neck down. Travis would never return to the ice. He would never add to the 11 seconds he spent on the ice as a player for Boston University.

He would later, though, regain some movement in his right arm.

This is a book about hockey, right? It might seem odd that given Travis' hockey journey came to such an abrupt end, anything inspirational could come from it.

It's not about what Travis did on the ice, but what he chose to do with the rest of his life that earns him a spot in this book. Because, you see, sometimes a bad break can inspire one to push forward and find a way to create positivity in the wake of tragedy.

In the next year after his injury, Travis founded the Travis Roy Foundation to promote awareness and raise funding for spinal cord injury survivors and research toward better treatments and cures. With his work for the Foundation moving forward, Travis continued his studies and graduated from Boston University in 2000, which was only one year behind his original timeline. His education could not be stopped by the injury.

Through those first few years of work with his foundation, Travis was honored by multiple hockey associations for his efforts. In 1996, the same year that Travis created his foundation, a new award was created in the state of Maine, a neighboring state of Massachusetts where Travis grew up and played high school hockey. The Travis Roy Award is now given to the best Class A high school hockey player in the state of Maine every year. Maine is a proud hockey state, so this is nothing short of a high honor in the hockey world. Young players in the state strive to collect that trophy every year.

In 1998, the North Yanmouth Academy's home ice rink was renamed to honor Travis Roy. The Travis Roy Arena also has Travis' number, 00, hanging in the rafters. If you are not familiar with hockey numbers displayed on a banner in the arena, it means that no other student to play for that school's team will ever be allowed to wear that number. It belongs to Travis. No matter what happens in that school moving forward, Travis's number will be a story passed down through generations.

In 1999, Boston University honored Travis by retiring his number, 24. It was the first time the University had ever retired a player's number, and it remained the only number retired until Travis' former coach, Jack Parker, received the same honor in 2014. Remember that these schools have great stories of hockey histories. Many of the best NHL players played for this school. They scored goals and made saves. They made spectacular plays and won championships. And yet, Travis and his coach are the only names and numbers in the rafters. Any student who plays hockey at the university will see that number hanging over them, and they will remember Travis and his journey.

Once his studies were finished, he did not sit back and work on the Foundation. He continued to look for ways to make a difference in the world. With many of his physical abilities now gone, he used one of the remaining physical abilities he had left: his voice.

Roy raised money for himself and the foundation by becoming a strong public speaker. He would appear in front of schools and businesses to share his story and inspire those who are going through difficulties. He learned how to deliver a message to people of all ages, showing how to persevere in the face of tragedy and pain.

As of today, the Travis Roy Foundation has awarded over $11 million to families to improve the quality of life for survivors, $25 million for paralyzed survivors, and more than $5 million for research funding.

It's not hard to see the inspiration in Travis Roy's story. He was hit with one of the worst setbacks anyone can imagine: not having the use of his physical body. But he was a hockey player. His mind was strong enough to deal with the pain and the loss. He used what he had left in his body to speak.

Sadly, Travis passed away at the age of 45, when complications from a recent surgery cut his life short. Although he is gone, his legacy will live on. His name and number will forever hang in the rafters of Boston University's hockey program, along with the banner in his high school hockey arena. His story will continue to inspire those who face hardship and need to know that they can still move forward. Travis Roy proved that even if hockey, and almost everything else, is taken away, greatness is still within reach.

Are your hardships or obstacles going to stop you, or are you going to use whatever strength you have left to push forward and make a positive difference?

STORY 3:

MARIO LEMIEUX'S RETURN

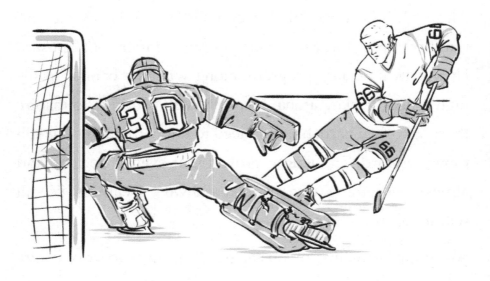

Few players in NHL history have had so significant of an impact on a single team as Mario Lemieux has had on the Pittsburgh Penguins. His life in the NHL began in 1984 when he was the first overall pick, thus beginning his career with the Penguins. Many Pittsburgh fans were hopeful that Lemieux could help the team in more ways than one. The organization had declared bankruptcy eight years before, and when Lemieux arrived, the team was only averaging around 7,000 fans in attendance, which was not even half of what their arena could hold.

Lemieux debuted in October 1984 when his team played the Boston Bruins, and he wasted no time making an impact. In his very first shift on the ice as a professional player, Lemieux stole a pass attempt away from future Hall-of-Famer Ray Bourque and skated in on a breakaway to score his first professional goal.

Of course, that was just the beginning of his greatness. While still in his rookie year, Lemieux was selected to play in the All-Star Game, which is quite the honor for a new player to the league. Even better, he was named the MVP of that game, the first rookie in NHL history to receive that distinction. To wrap up his opening campaign, Lemieux tallied 100 points and received the Calder Trophy, which is

21

awarded to the league's top rookie at the end of each season.

In his sophomore campaign, Lemieux scored a whopping 141 points, which was second only to Wayne Gretzky, who broke the NHL record with 215 points. The NHL players voted Lemieux as the best regular-season player that year, too. Still accelerating his scoring pace, he scored 168 points in the 1987-1988 season, which was the highest by any player that year.

Needless to say, Mario Lemieux, or Super Mario, as he would come to be known, was crushing the league at every opportunity. His best personal performance, though, was still yet to come. In the 1988-1989 season, Lemieux set an NHL record by being the only player to score a goal in each of the five possible game situations in a single game: even strength, power play, shorthanded, penalty shot, and empty net. He also ended that season with 199 points, making him the only player besides Gretzky to ever come close to a 200-point season.

Fighting through severe back pain that included a herniated disc surgery, Lemieux scored 44 points in the 1990-1991 playoffs to help the Penguins win their first-ever Stanley Cup as champions of the league. He was awarded the Conn

Smythe Trophy as the MVP of the playoffs as well. With a championship under his belt, Lemieux fought through more injuries and helped the Penguins repeat as Stanley Cup Champions in the 1991-1992 season, winning another MVP trophy as well.

At this point, Mario Lemieux likely had a hockey resume worthy of the Hall of Fame. Two Stanley Cups, multiple scoring titles, and a franchise brought back from the brink of destruction. But, somehow, his 1992-1993 season started even stronger! Lemieux set a franchise record by scoring a goal in every single one of the first 12 games of the season. Throughout the first half of the season, he was setting a pace to challenge Wayne Gretzky's records for most goals and points in a single season until he made an announcement that shocked the hockey world.

Mario Lemieux had been diagnosed with Hodgkin's lymphoma. What followed was two months of missed hockey as he underwent aggressive radiation treatments. Remember that this was in January 1993, and while cancer treatments are always improving, they were hardly a sure thing at that time. It was grueling and tiring, but Mario continued to fight on.

But, as the greatest hockey players young and old have shown, they never back down from a challenge. They never quit. And after two months of misery, doubts, and fears, and 22 missed games, Mario Lemieux surprised the hockey world, and even his teammates, by returning to the lineup on March 2, 1993, to help his team against the Philadelphia Flyers. What is truly amazing about his return is that his last cancer treatment had been earlier that same day! Mario Lemieux truly was Super Mario.

When he took to the ice in Philadelphia, hockey fans watching from home in Pittsburgh were thrilled to see their captain back on the ice. What those Pittsburgh fans did not expect, though, was how the Philadelphia Flyers fans in the arena would react to his return. If you've ever been to a hockey game, or any sport, for that matter, you may have witnessed, or taken part in, some booing of the opponents. It's a fun part of being a spectator for many fans. And, if your team happens to be playing against a rival team, you might expect that booing to be even louder. Make no mistake. Pittsburgh and Philadelphia were rivals. Pittsburgh fans watching at home expected the normal boos.

When Mario's name was announced for the starting lineups, the fans in that arena did what most thought they would never do for their cross-state rival. Every fan in that building got up from their seat and applauded Mario Lemieux. The moment was tear-jerking for any who witnessed it.

Mario Lemieux would tally one goal and one assist in that game. For the rest of the season, Lemieux continued to play at a level higher than any other player in the league. Despite missing those 22 games, he still won the NHL scoring title for that season with 160 points in 60 games.

The greatness that Mario displayed through injury and cancer is inspiration at its core. The mental toughness to overcome what he did, not knowing his fate, and the physical toughness to go through cancer treatments, and then return to play with a back injury always nagging at him, it is all the stuff of hockey legends.

Lemieux retired in 1996. Somehow, though, the team he left would need to be rescued once more. The Pittsburgh Penguins overspent in the 90s, and when they stopped winning, they could not pay their debts. Over the summer and fall of 1998, Mario Lemieux became the majority owner of the team when he used much of his deferred salary to purchase equity in the team. He promised to keep the team from folding, and also made sure that the team would stay in Pittsburgh. It was the first time in NHL history that a former player became the majority owner of a team.

After retiring and becoming the owner of the only NHL team he ever played for, Mario Lemieux's story came to an end.

Just kidding! Mario's young son wished he could see his father play. Super Mario was also a super dad, so he rejoined the Pittsburgh Penguins in December 2000. He played in 43 games that season and totaled 76 points, which was good enough for 26th place in scoring. Let's pause here for just a moment to consider that stat. Mario Lemieux was *retired*. He hadn't played since the spring of 1996! But because his son wanted him to, Mario returned to play half of an NHL season. Every other player had the opportunity to play 82 games. He played 43. Still, only 25 players accumulated more points than he did that year.

As the only player-owner in the NHL, Mario Lemieux had the opportunity to make decisions for the team's direction going forward. There are many trades, signings, and developing players that could be discussed here, but only one is really worth mentioning. In the summer of 2005, Mario Lemieux and the Pittsburgh Penguins drafted a young Canadian player named Sidney Crosby as the first overall pick. If you haven't heard of him, he's led the Penguins to three more Stanley Cups. But, back to the real hero of the story.

In January 2006, Mario Lemieux retired again, for good this time. He was now 40 years old and suffering from atrial fibrillation, which is when your heart doesn't beat correctly. After 22 years of helping the Pittsburgh Penguins in every way he could, Mario finally hung up the skates and focused on the duties of ownership.

As part-owner, Mario Lemieux, along with the aforementioned Sidney Crosby, has helped the Penguins win three more championships, cementing them as one of the NHL's powerhouse franchises. Quite the turnaround from a decade earlier! The team is financially strong, nowhere near the two bankruptcies of the past, and the city of Pittsburgh is better for it. In every way, Mario Lemieux's career has been super, and that is an inspiration to all hockey fans, not just those who like wearing the yellow and black of the Penguins.

STORY 4:

THE FIRST ALL-STAR GAME

When a 'hockey fan' thinks of the NHL All-Star Game, they think of a fun-filled weekend full of skill competitions, nods to hockey history and the best players in the world gathered together to play a fun, entertaining game for the fans. What many may not think about, though, is how such an annual tradition came to be. After all, an annual event had to have an inaugural event first.

So, how did the All-Star Game come to the NHL? Well, that is a complicated but very inspirational story.

The story begins with a Canadian NHL player by the name of Ace Bailey.

Irvine Wallace Bailey (known as Ace) was born in Ontario, Canada, way back in 1903. He grew up playing hockey, and his first junior team was Toronto St. Mary's, which was part of the Ontario Hockey Association. He then played a couple of seasons of senior hockey in Peterborough before becoming a professional hockey player for the Toronto Maple Leafs. He spent eight seasons with that team, from 1926-1933.

During that time, Ace Bailey gained a reputation in the league for being a smooth skater with deft control of the puck. He was also a great penalty killer and was often utilized in those situations during games.

You may have noticed that eight years is not a full-length career. Ace Bailey, unfortunately, had his career cut short by a serious physical injury on December 12, 1933, when he was just 30 years old. The Toronto Maple Leafs and Boston Bruins met in a clash that would be remembered for decades. These were two teams built with tough players in every position. The teams' owners -Art Ross of the Bruins and Conn Smythe of the Leafs - hated each other just as much as the teams' players hated each other.

When it came to rivalries, early hockey had a ton of them because there were very few teams. That meant that teams saw quite a bit of each other over a season.

Before a description of the injury, it's important to remember that hockey back in the early years of the sport was much more physical. There was more hitting, punching, slashing, and all of the things that today's hockey has eliminated from the game. With that, let's take a look at what happened to Ace Bailey.

It all began during that game on December 12, when Maple Leafs player King Clancy threw a punishing hit on Eddie

Shore of the Boston Bruins. The hit rattled Shore and dazed him a bit, and when he got back on his skates, he was angry and looking to return the favor against Clancy. Skating back up the ice as fast as he could, Shore targeted his man and hit him from behind, sending the player to the ice. Unfortunately, that player was not King Clancy; it was Ace Bailey. Even worse, Bailey's head hit the ice, and the impact caused a severe injury. Bailey's skull bone had fractured.

As Bailey lay on the ice, suffering convulsions from the injury, players around him took care of business. Red Horner of the Leafs knocked out Shore with one punch to the jaw.

Ace Bailey was taken to the hospital in Boston, where many doctors thought that he would not survive. Bailey went into two separate comas over two weeks, and he underwent several operations while he was hospitalized. Ultimately, Bailey survived the incident, but his family was left to pay the massive bills that were piling up from the medical care.

The league suspended Eddie Shore for 16 games, which was a third of a season back in 1933. But the league also wanted to find a way to help Ace Bailey's family handle those medical bills. As the league searched for a solution, they gained inspiration from professional baseball.

31

Coincidentally, just the summer before, on July 6, 1933, Major League Baseball held its first All-Star Game in Chicago.

With another league having success with the concept, the National Hockey League thought they would give it a shot, though they tweaked a couple of details. First, they would collect the best players from all of the other teams to play against the Maple Leafs. Second, all of the proceeds from the game's tickets would be donated to Ace Bailey's family to help with his medical bills.

It is amazing that players from all over the league would come together and play a game to benefit someone who was in need. This is the first token of inspiration from this story, that the league and its players found a way to support one of their own. Even if they wore different jerseys and had fierce battles against one another, they could still find the humanity in helping Ace Bailey and his family.

As for the game itself, it took place on February 14, 1934, at the Maple Leafs' home arena, Maple Leaf Gardens. Ironically, Eddie Shore had completed his suspension by this time and was selected to play in the game. We might look at this decision today and wonder how Shore wasn't barred from competing ever again, or how he wasn't held out of the game since his actions directly caused the league to implement the All-Star Game - but these were different times. In fact, the true moment of inspiration would come during the game itself.

It was reported that Shore was quite uncomfortable with the idea of playing in this game, as he still felt enormous guilt over his actions. However, his discomfort would be eased by the most unlikely of individuals: Ace Bailey.

As the players warmed up and took their practice shots before the game was set to begin, the league held a pre-game ceremony to mark the occasion. Each player was presented with a commemorative jacket and medals, but the real shock was that Ace Bailey himself had walked out into the arena to hand out those tokens of commemoration himself.

The applause from the audience was described as a roar. To see Bailey recovering, able to walk on his own, and getting better every day, brought inspiration to the fans and the players. When Eddie Shore stepped up to receive his medal and jacket from Bailey, the two men looked at each other for a moment and then shook hands. They shared a few private words, both smiling before the rest of the ceremony proceeded.

There was no condemnation, animosity, or blame. The two men did not shout at each other or make a scene. They didn't roll their eyes or give a sarcastic shrug. That moment of forgiveness is one that should be celebrated widely in the hockey world. Perhaps there should be a little bit of room for forgiveness in today's world.

At the end of the ceremony, the Maple Leafs' Conn Smythe presented Ace Bailey with a commemorative jersey of his own. Smythe also announced to Bailey and the rest of the arena that Bailey's number six would never be worn by another Toronto player. He was the first professional player to have his number retired.

As for the result of the game, the Maple Leafs defeated the All-Stars by a score of 7-3. The event raised over $20,000 for Bailey and his family.

Eddie Shore commented to reporters after the game that he was surprised when the crowd cheered for him a few different times during the contest. It was almost as if the entire city of Toronto had also forgiven him for what had happened.

This sort of sportsmanship likely would not have happened in today's hockey world. Terrible hits create lifelong enemies for teams and their fans. But, in this instance, there were a couple of distinct differences: Ace Bailey spoke with Eddie Shore and shook his hand. Also, Eddie Shore expressed remorse for what he had done. Accepting responsibility for his actions allowed Shore to receive forgiveness.

While this All-Star Game was not considered the first official NHL All-Star Game, it did set the precedent for the sport to try it in the future. More importantly, though, it showed the players and fans that humanity is more important than the war on the ice.

As for Ace Bailey, he tried a few different ways to incorporate himself back into the NHL. First, he tried to become a linesman, but he was not permitted to do so. Next, the Maple Leafs had a trophy made that bore his name, which he delivered to the NHL president. Bailey's idea was that the trophy could be awarded to All-Star Game winners in the future and that proceeds from those games would benefit injured players. However, that idea was also declined.

Ace Bailey did find a spot as a coach for the University of Toronto for several years, winning three Canadian Interuniversity Athletics Union championships in that time.

Furthermore, he worked as a timekeeper for the Maple Leafs' home games.

Ace has left a legacy of forgiveness and tenacity. He would not give up on the world of hockey, always looking to make a difference in whatever way he could. He also did not hold a grudge against the man who ended his professional hockey career. Instead, he used the moment to demonstrate that humanity is bigger than hockey.

STORY 5:

PAUL KARIYA'S ICONIC MOMENT

Few NHL players have solidified their careers with an iconic moment that did not involve a Stanley Cup Championship. Paul Kariya is one of those few. He never won a Stanley Cup, but he did create moments that fans will remember forever. Let's take a look at one specific moment that will inspire any player to get back up whenever they get knocked down, no matter how hard they hit the ice. But first, let's take a look at Paul's story as a whole.

Paul Kariya was born in Vancouver, British Columbia in 1974. He had athletic genetics, as his father played rugby for the Canadian national team. Paul turned to hockey at a young age, though, and he didn't look back. He played two years of Junior A hockey with the Penticton Panthers, and he was named the Junior A Player of the Year in his second year there.

He then attended the University of Maine and played one year of college hockey. In that one year, Kariya garnered a ton of national attention. He won the Hobey Baker Award, granted to the top NCAA hockey player every year, and his team won the NCAA title in that same season. That next summer, Kariya was selected fourth overall by the Anaheim Mighty Ducks.

Paul Kariya's professional career, although it lacks a Stanley Cup, is littered with accolades and awards that were very well deserved. In his first season, he was named to the NHL All-Rookie team. He went on to win two Lady Byng Trophies in 1996 and '97 for gentlemanly play, along with gold medals when he represented Canada at the 1994 World Championships in Italy and the 2002 Olympics at Salt Lake City.

He was, by all accounts, a very successful NHL player. In fact, his career was so decorated that he was voted into the Hockey Hall of Fame in 2017, and his number nine was retired by the Anaheim Ducks in 2018. Few players in NHL history are so honored by the sport and the team they play for, so these two accolades speak volumes about Kariya's success on the ice.

In this story, though, we're going to focus on one pivotal moment in his career that might help you more accurately understand how he was so successful. It will assist you to see just how tenacious and relentless he was. After all, it's easy to list his accomplishments and forget that before every success was an obstacle or a failure that threatened to derail his career.

Paul Kariya made it to the Stanley Cup Finals just one time in a professional career that lasted 16 years. In the 2002-2003 season, the Anaheim Ducks made the playoffs as the seventh of eight seeds in the Western Conference, which is a very low seed. Kariya struggled to score goals during the season, as he only tallied 25. He did, though, notch 56 assists and earn his seventh All-Star nomination. Even though low seeds have a statistically lower chance to advance through the tournament, it has happened before, and the Ducks wanted it to happen again.

As for the playoff run itself, his team had an uphill battle that started with a series against the defending Stanley Cup Champion Detroit Red Wings. The Ducks, though, were out to prove that they should not be underestimated, even by the defending champs. Kariya himself scored the game-winning goal in triple overtime of the first game of the series, setting the tone for his team and coming up tops when they needed it. The Ducks would go on to sweep the Wings in four straight games, putting the rest of the league on notice.

The Ducks' winning ways would continue with their captain, Paul Kariya, leading the way despite playing several games with a separated shoulder. It's important to pause and consider the seriousness of that injury. A player needs his shoulders working properly to do anything on the ice. Want to hit? Hope your shoulder can take the impact. Want to pass or shoot? Hope your shoulders can rotate through the movement. Paul Kariya, though, would not be denied.

The Ducks defeated the top-ranked Dallas Stars in six games, including a five-overtime win in Game 1. In the Western Conference Final, Kariya and the Ducks swept the Minnesota Wild to earn a trip to the Stanley Cup Final. Waiting for them were the New Jersey Devils, a team full of veterans, many of whom had won Stanley Cups in the past.

The series was a battle. Each team held serve on their home ice as the series bounced back and forth across the country. In Game 6, the game was in Anaheim, and the Ducks needed to win if they wanted a chance to win the cup in Game 7.

And this is the scene for Paul Kariya's defining moment. In the second period of Game 6, Anaheim had a 3-1 lead with just over 13 minutes left in the frame. The teams were playing tight, physical hockey, and so far, the bounces had gone the Ducks' way. It looked as though that would continue when Kariya intercepted a pass attempt from Scott Gomez of the Devils. Kariya turned at center ice and began skating toward the Devils' blue line when he passed the puck to his left. He turned right but continued to watch his pass until Scott Stevens, all 215 pounds of him, hit Paul Kariya and sent him down to the ice.

The Ducks bench exploded in protests as the play was immediately blown dead, as Kariya was not initially moving after the hit. A close-up camera angle shows Kariya's face, and you can clearly see the moment he takes his first breath because it fogs up the visor on his helmet that was pushed down from the hit.

Fans were angry and players were angry, but no penalty was called on the play. Kariya was able to get to his feet, where he was guided to the dressing room for further evaluation. Fans in the arena were upset and anxious. Their captain was injured, and from the looks of the hit, most assumed that he would not return.

But Paul Kariya was playing as an inspired hockey player. He was in the dressing room for approximately ten minutes, only four and a half minutes had gone by in the game time. After that, he returned to the bench and was ready to go. The fans in the arena cheered when they realized that he had returned to the game. His teammates, undoubtedly, felt better knowing that he was not severely injured. His presence was a boost to everyone around him.

To return from a hit as violent as that would take a lot of grit. Paul Kariya had it. And, of course, the story could end there. But, it doesn't.

With just under three minutes to play in the second period, Kariya was on the ice and streaking up the neutral zone when a pass came his way. He caught it, and because he was moving so quickly, the Devils' defensemen had to give him more room than normal, as they did not want to get beaten to the outside. This gave Kariya time to enter the offensive zone unharassed, and he wound up for a slapshot as he glided toward the top of the faceoff circle to the left of Devils goaltender Martin Brodeur, who himself would soon be in the Hall of Fame.

What happened next is one of the most goosebump-inducing moments in hockey history, and it was aided by the television broadcast play-by-play announcer, Gary Thorne.

When Kariya accepted the pass and began skating into the zone, Gary Thorne could sense the immediate buzz in the arena, and in the one free moment he had, Thorne said, "Kariya, the fans want one…"

Paul Kariya wound up and released a slapshot aiming for Brodeur's glove side, and the puck absolutely blew by the goaltender. It rippled the mesh netting, and the fans in the arena exploded in cheers.

Gary Thorne put a pin on the moment when he yelled, "SCOOOOORE! OFF THE FLOOR, ON THE BOARD, PAUL KARIYA!"

Kariya yelled with passion as his teammates circled him in celebration, the goal horn sounding off as the fans continued to yell and cheer to show their approval. It was the moment of the series, without question. Fans of the Ducks would talk about that goal for years to come.

The Ducks would go on to win Game 6 convincingly, setting up a Game 7, winner-take-all showdown back in New Jersey.

Unfortunately, Paul Kariya would not win a Stanley Cup, as the Devils held serve on their home ice and won Game 7. Not a fitting ending to his story, but it shows how big the moment was. Even though the Ducks didn't win, that moment still endures as a legend.

Kariya would not make it back to the Stanley Cup Final for the rest of his career, which ended officially in 2011 when he announced that his history of concussions would prevent him from playing any longer. Undoubtedly, one of those concussions took place during this event, but these injuries were not as closely tracked as they are in today's game, in which Kariya would not have been permitted to return to the ice so quickly.

Even though the storybook ending did not come to pass for Kariya and his team, that moment in Game 6 of the 2003 Stanley Cup Final will live on for generations. To see the grit and tenacity in real-time, to see a man wholly defeated, but then return to have his triumphant victory is inspiring to all those who face challenges and hardship in their lives.

You may suffer defeat as Paul Kariya once did, but you always have the opportunity to get back up and prove that defeat is not permanent. You can prove that your story will not be defined by your losses, but by your ability to stand back up and fight for another shot at success.

GORDIE HOWE'S CONTINUED EXCELLENCE

One source of inspiration comes from longevity, especially when it comes to exceeding the expectations put on you by the world and society around you. As you, dear reader, get older and progress through life, you might discover that your older, aging body is no longer able to do the things it was capable of when you were youthful and energetic. It is inspirational, then, when you witness an immensely talented athlete continue to compete for much longer than the average player.

This story is about Gordie Howe, or Mr. Hockey, as many refer to him these days. His name is well known to hockey fans and historians for many reasons, so let's take a look at some of his spectacular accomplishments before we examine just how he was able to play professional hockey for a record six separate decades. Yes, that's right! We're about to embark on a hockey career that spanned from the 1940s to the 1990s. In all of hockey history, this player is the only one to do it.

Gordie Howe was born in 1928, in Saskatchewan, Canada, where he lived on a farm with his parents and eight siblings. Growing up on a farm is not an easy life, and it is possible that this upbringing helped prepare him for the battles that he would wage on the ice. He played some youth hockey with the King George Athletic Club in Saskatoon before being invited to training camp with the New York Rangers when he was just 15 years old.

After the training camp, the Rangers offered Howe one year of hockey at Notre Dame, a prestigious university in the United States, in exchange for the Rangers having the rights to sign Howe to their team if he entered the league. This, already, is an amazing accomplishment for a young hockey player. Unlike other sports where young players are scouted early on, such as soccer teams around the world, this did not happen in hockey back then. So, to see someone get an offer like that at age 15 is truly special. It shows just how skilled Gordie Howe already was at such a young age. The Rangers knew he was a talent.

Let's take a moment so you can consider what you would decide to do in this situation. You're 15 years old, not even done with school. Your family needs help on the farm at home because times are tough, but the New York Rangers are offering to put you into Notre Dame for college hockey, and then they'll draft you if you develop well. Maybe you'll make it into the league, or maybe you won't, but you'll get an education out of it either way. And if the Rangers lose interest, maybe they sell your rights to another team.

Would you take that offer? Young Gordie had a lot to think about at that moment.

Ultimately, Gordie Howe determined that he would rather stay in Canada and play hockey with his friends. He also wanted to help his family on the farm, so he turned down the Rangers' offer. Imagine that! Imagine being 15 years old and turning down an opportunity to get one foot into the door of an NHL organization.

So, if he turned down the NHL at this point, what was the path he ended up taking?

One year later, after Howe had just turned down the Rangers, he was noticed by another NHL team. The Detroit Red Wings had a scout named Fred Pinkney, and he invited Howe to Detroit's training camp in Windsor, Ontario. If you're not familiar with the geography of Canada, Windsor is just across the Detroit River from the city of Detroit, so to have the team practicing in Canada was not abnormal.

Howe decided to sign with this team, ultimately, and his NHL career was ever closer to its beginning.

The Red Wings assigned Howe to the Galt Red Wings, the junior team affiliated with the Red Wings organization, where Howe played for one year before being promoted to the Omaha Knights of the United States Hockey League. In his first season there, as a 17-year-old, Howe tallied 48 points in 51 games.

That fall, Gordie was inserted into the Red Wings' lineup, and he played his first game for the team on October 16, 1946. Now, we could spend a long time going over Gordie Howe's accomplishments in the NHL, but I'll focus on just a couple you've heard about, and maybe one or two you haven't.

Gordie Howe currently ranks third in all-time goals and fourth in all-time points. He won four Stanley Cups with the Red Wings, and he led the team to seven consecutive first-place regular season finishes, a feat that has never been matched since. Another feat unmatched by any other player is that Howe finished in the top five of scoring every year for 20 straight seasons. It is important to note, though, that Gordie Howe was competing in a league that had only six teams until 1968 when it expanded to 12. But, for good measure, Gordie tallied 103 points in the second season of the expansion.

When Gordie Howe was forced to retire due to a lingering wrist injury at the age of 43, he took a job in the Red Wings' front office, but it was short-lived. He was unhappy with not having much of an impact on the organization, so when the Houston Aeros of the brand-new World Hockey Association came knocking with a contract offer to play for them, he decided to take it.

Gordie played with Houston from 1974 to 1977, when he joined another team in the WHA, the New England Whalers. He played two seasons there before the WHA folded, and the New England Whalers became the Hartford Whalers, who joined the NHL. The Red Wings still had Howe's rights, but they agreed not to claim Gordie away from Hartford.

Even though Gordie had been done with the NHL, he ended up back in the league again!

Gordie played until the end of the 1979-1980 season when he retired once more. He had played professional hockey across four decades! No matter your age, this would be quite a goal to reach for, even if you never make it to the professional ranks.

Before Gordie hung up the skates forever, he was signed to a one-day contract by the Detroit Vipers of the International Hockey League. He skated one shift in one game, at age 69, becoming the only player in professional hockey history to play across five decades! From 1946 to 1997, Gordie's professional career spanned 51 years.

Many of the readers looking through these stories will not have reached the age of 51 yet, let alone understand the limitations on the human body at the age of 69, but Gordie Howe was not held back by such limitations. If there is an inspirational idea to take from this story, it is that Gordie Howe loved the game of hockey, and he didn't let the limitation of time prevent him from enjoying the game he loved. Other stories in this book talk about players overcoming disease, injury, and personal loss. Those are terrible tragedies that are difficult to recover from. But the one thing that no one can defeat is time.

Gordie Howe fought against time itself, and he did better than any other professional hockey player had ever done in that arena. There was no obstacle that Gordie Howe wouldn't face head-on during his career, and time was no different. Consider that the next time you're facing an insurmountable obstacle, one that seems naturally unbeatable. You might think, "There's no point in fighting because I can't win." Gordie Howe's story would argue back and point out that sometimes fighting back, even if you ultimately lose, is still worth the battle. It is still worth proving that you are tough and can do more than others could.

You never know until you give it a shot.

STORY 7:

SAKU KOIVU BATTLES BACK

There are times when you might think that the odds are stacked against you. Maybe, you think, there's a higher power who doesn't want to help you, or that karma is giving you a bad shake, and that you're just not destined for the dreams you once held in your heart. You might see friends and family around you who don't have a lot of problems to deal with as you do, and you're a little jealous of the ease they get to experience. You might be angry and just feel like giving up some days, thinking that a path with less danger might be the way you are meant to go. This is a story about someone who would not be moved by bad luck, even after years of it.

This story follows one player by the name of Saku Koivu. When it comes to catching some very bad breaks, Koivu's career and personal story rank among some of the worst streaks of luck and injury in hockey history, but he never gave up on his passion for the game. Let's take a look at Koivu's journey through the NHL and all that it entailed, and maybe you'll understand that you're not the only one who has several hurdles to jump and that there's always a path forward for you to pursue.

Saku Koivu was drafted 21st overall in the 1993 draft by the Montreal Canadiens. Before coming over to North America to play in the NHL, he spent two more seasons with his SM-liiga team, Turun Palloseura. After entering the NHL in the 1995-1996 season, he scored 45 points in 82 games. In his second season, he was high up in the NHL scoring ranks on the season until he suffered a knee injury against Chicago and missed 32 games. He returned at the end of the season and added 18 more points to finish with 56 in only 50 games. This is quite impressive, considering that knee injuries can greatly impact how a player skates on the ice.

That's one hurdle he overcame, and you can probably guess that it wouldn't be the last.

In the 1997-1998 season, he suffered more leg injuries and missed 13 games. But 57 points in 69 games is still good. The next year, more injuries caused him to miss 17 games. He scored 44 points in 65 games.

Let's call that another hurdle, even if the injuries were partial. Remember that the human body doesn't improve as it gets older, so these injuries would likely continue to pile up until Koivu's body would give out from the stress.

At this point, it must have been frustrating to be so close to having it all in the hockey world. Everyone knew Koivu was a special player, but he couldn't catch a break. Surely it would come soon, and he would win a scoring title and lead his team on a deep playoff run, right?

Well, some good news did come his way. Even though he struggled with injuries, Montreal knew he was talented. They named him the new captain of the team after Vincent Damphousse left the team. Unfortunately, his first season as the captain of the Montreal Canadiens did not go well. Koivu suffered a dislocated shoulder and was forced to miss 40 games, nearly half of a season. After that, everything was fine.

Just kidding!

When he returned from the injury, he injured his knee...again. His first season as captain came to an end after he had only played 24 games.

His second season as the captain would be better, right? Well, slightly. Remember those knee injuries? Well, doctors decided that Koivu needed arthroscopic surgery on his left knee. He missed 28 games and scored 47 points on the season.

Let's call this batch of injuries another hurdle. Hopefully, by this point, you can see that Koivu has had a bad shake of an NHL career so far. What's truly frustrating is that Koivu was massively talented and a natural goal-scorer when he could be on the ice. But his career would turn around.

Just kidding, again!

On a plane ride from Finland back to North America before the start of the 2001-2002 season, Koivu's teammate, Brian Savage, noticed that Koivu looked pale. Koivu had been suffering from severe stomach pain and vomiting, which prompted him to visit the team doctor, David Mulder. After dozens of tests, Mulder had found the source of Saku Koivu's troubles, and it wasn't the flu. Koivu was diagnosed with Burkitt's lymphoma.

Cancer.

His diagnosis was confirmed on September 6, 2001, and he was scheduled to miss the entire season as he underwent treatment.

Here's another hurdle that he had to overcome. Do you think he would have been justified in giving up on a professional hockey career? Would anyone blame him for deciding that he had to put his physical health first and go into a line of work that wasn't actively trying to remove him from the planet?

It's unlikely that anyone would have judged him for retiring from the game of hockey.

Spoiler: he didn't retire.

In fact, he did what many considered to be impossible. He made it through his treatments faster than anticipated, and he stayed in shape the entire time he was off the ice. Any professional athlete will tell you that if you do not get to play for an extended period, it's difficult to get back up to the speed of the game. But, Koivu would not give up, no matter how many hurdles were thrown his way. On April 9, 2002, he returned to the ice for Montreal's final three games of the season.

In his first game back, the crowd in Montreal's arena, the Molson Centre, stood and cheered in preparation for their team to take the ice, knowing that Koivu was among their ranks. The sound from the arena was nearly deafening, even when heard from the locker room. As the team filed down the hallway, the cheers continued. And when Saku Koivu's skates touched the ice, the cheering swelled to an eruption of sound.

Koivu skated around the ice and took in the scene. He looked on as thousands and thousands of fans stood and cheered for him nonstop through the entire warmup time. They even continued cheering through the national anthem. The announcers thought they might get a word in - then his name was announced as the starting center for the game, which set off the eruption of cheering once more. In total, the crowd stood and cheered for eight minutes.

Think of the last time you saw a performance that earned a standing ovation. Maybe a school band or choir, or perhaps a play. Did the crowd stand and cheer for eight minutes? Likely not.

Koivu had cleared every devastating hurdle and obstacle thrown his way. He deserved every second of that eight minutes. Even better, though, is that Saku Koivu and the Montreal Canadiens went on to clinch a playoff spot for that season. Somehow, even better than that, the eighth-seeded Montreal Canadiens defeated the top-seeded Boston Bruins in the first round of the playoffs.

While the Canadiens did not win the Stanley Cup, many considered their run in 2002 to be quite successful, and they were happy to have Saku Koivu back in their lineup. At the end of the season, Koivu was awarded the Bill Masterson Memorial Trophy, which is awarded every year to the player who best demonstrates the following qualities:

perseverance, dedication, and sportsmanship in the game of ice hockey.

In fact, if you're looking for more inspirational stories, looking at the list of past winners of the Bill Masterson Memorial Trophy would be a good place to start.

After the 2002 season, Koivu missed 12 more games from more knee issues, but otherwise had a couple of successful years without major issues. Unfortunately, that did not last. In the 2006 playoffs, Koivu was hit in the face with a high stick that caused a serious injury to his left eye. Koivu was taken to the nearby hospital immediately, and he remained in the hospital's care for the rest of the playoffs.

He eventually had surgery to fix the detached retina in his eye, and the result left him missing some of his peripheral vision, meaning that he couldn't as much out of the corner of his eye. He also had a cataract form in his eye, which also had to be removed by doctors.

More hurdles, but Koivu would not be deterred.

In the next season, Koivu tallied a career-high 75 points. Even more importantly, he played in 81 of the 82 regular season games, which he had done only one other time in his career.

After every hurdle, Koivu still turned in a fantastic season, especially considering what he had dealt with over that period. With several leg and knee injuries, cancer, and an eye injury, Saku Koivu defied the odds and found a way to make it work.

He even suffered a broken foot in the 2008 playoffs but was still able to tally nine points over seven games. There was also the criticism he received from Guy Bertrand, a nationalist lawyer who was not happy that the captain of the Montreal Canadiens did not speak French, which is the preferred language in Montreal. Well, Koivu brushed up on his French and re-taped a pre-game video for the arena where he said, *"Ici Saku Koivu, voici mon equipe."* When translated into English, it means, "Saku Koivu here, this is my team."

Seems like a foreign language was no match for Saku Koivu, either. Add it to the list of foes that Koivu had defeated over the years.

So, how does this story end? Well, Saku Koivu played professional hockey for 18 years. He played in 1,124 NHL games in total, scoring 255 goals and earning 577 assists, for a total of 832 points. He also played in 79 playoff games, where he had 60 points. Those are very good numbers for a professional hockey player, especially when one considers all of the obstacles that he had to overcome.

Most players in that situation would have left the game. Or, their list of injuries would have prevented them from keeping a spot on an NHL roster. An injury or two would have made a significant negative impact on their game, and they would have faded from the world of professional hockey. It happens all the time. Saku Koivu worked hard to keep up his skill and fitness to maintain his career over anything that tried to get in the way.

The next time you're feeling that the obstacles in your life are too much to overcome, or if you feel that breaks never go your way, remember that it is possible. It is always possible to find the strength and perseverance to continue. Saku Koivu found a way to push through it all and have a great, inspirational hockey career.

STORY 8:

THE '97-'98 DETROIT
RED WINGS

The story of the 1997-'98 Detroit Red Wings is one which begins at the end of the previous season. In June 1997, the Detroit Red Wings were facing off in the Stanley Cup Final against the Philadelphia Flyers. For the Red Wings, it had been 42 years since their last championship, and the fans of that team had gone through decades of disappointment.

But the Red Wings had a team brimming with players that would eventually end up in the Hall of Fame. Captain Steve Yzerman, Nicklas Lidstrom, Brendan Shanahan, Larry Murphy, and Sergei Fedorov are just some of the highlights. One of the biggest staples of the team was a line of players known as the Russian Five. This included Sergei Fedorov, Igor Larionov, Slava Kozlov, Slava Fetisov, and Vladimir Konstantinov.

For the first time in NHL history, five Russian-born players had taken to the ice together on October 27, 1995, and Red Wings coach Scotty Bowman elected to play them together often over the next few years. Fetisov and Konstantinov were physical defensemen while Larionov as the centerman had great vision to feed passes to the speedy and talented wingers, Kozlov and Fedorov. The combination was lethal, and something unseen in the league to that point.

This background is important, though, because the story of the 1997-1998 Detroit Red Wings is going to center on Vladimir Konstantinov, the hard-hitting defenseman.

Back to June 1997 and the Stanley Cup Finals between the Red Wings and the Flyers. Over four games, the Red Wings outscored the Flyers 16 to 6, including many long-range slap shots and a beautiful goal from enforcer Darren McCarty, and they went on to win the Stanley Cup in four straight games.

One of the best images from that series was from Vladimir Konstantinov, who delivered a punishing hit on Dale Hawerchuk. It was an iconic moment, as it happened at center ice, over the winged wheel painted on the ice surface, and the Detroit crowd was electrified with excitement by the play.

The party was on with that Stanley Cup victory not only in Detroit but also around the entire state of Michigan. The team had not won the Cup since 1955, so the players and fans undoubtedly celebrated wildly for many days after the final game on June 7, 1997.

That party would come to an abrupt end just six days later.

After a golf outing with the Cup on display, defensemen Slava Fetisov and Vladimir Konstantinov, along with the team's masseur, Sergei Mnatsakanov, hired a limousine to drive them back from the golf course to their homes. What they did not know was that the man driving that limousine had a suspended license for drunk driving. Unfortunately, they did not make it home that night, as the limousine crashed into a tree.

Images of the damaged limousine were shown on local and sports news channels around the hockey world. The Red Wings were devastated, and it was reported at the time that players, coaches, and members of the team's management all visited the injured players in the hospital quite often.

Fetisov managed to emerge with minor injuries. Both Mnatsakanov and Konstantinov suffered severe injuries, and they both spent time in multiple comas in the days just after. The team, the fans, and the city were in mourning for their teammates.

As Sergei and Vladimir began their recovery processes, the team rallied around them to offer love and support.

The players decided that they would dedicate the upcoming season to both of these individuals, so they had a patch designed and sewn into all of their jerseys. They were circular, with the Red Wing on the top third. Under the Red Wing was a waving banner that said "Believe" in both English and Russian, and under the banner were the initials of the two injured members of the organization. But they wanted to do more than just put a patch on their jerseys. They wanted to show their injured friends how much they cared for them. They wanted to win another Stanley Cup to present to them at the end of the season.

What better way to show a hockey player you care for them than to win the most difficult trophy in all of the professional sports?

That is the stage for the 1997-1998 Detroit Red Wings. But, just how much of a season could this team put together with such an emotional weight on their shoulders? Let's take a look.

Throughout the regular season, the Red Wings scored 250 goals in 82 games, which ranked second in the league. They gave up 196 goals, which was seventh-best. Captain Steve Yzerman led the team in scoring with 69 points. With that performance, the Red Wings earned the third seed in the Western Conference as they headed into the playoffs.

But what was working against them? Well, besides having to fill the large gap left by Konstantinov's absence, the team also played the majority of the regular season without Sergei Fedorov, who was holding out for a contract offer after he had signed an offer sheet from the Carolina Hurricanes worth $38 million, which included bonuses.

For reference, the playoffs began on April 22, but Fedorov had only joined the roster at the end of February. Still, his skill and speed would be a great help come playoff time.

Besides, they had been down one of their Hall-of-Fame forwards but still managed to finish in third place in the conference. Many analysts and pundits picked them as favorites to repeat as champions, but the path to the trophy is still long, and many things can go wrong along the way. And they did.

Another worry entering the playoffs was the team's performance on the road. While they had a record of 25-8-8 at home, they were a very pedestrian 19-15-7 on the road. Many hockey analysts will tell you that the key to winning in the playoffs is finding ways to win on the road.

Their first-round opponent was the Phoenix Coyotes. After an opening 6-3 victory on home ice, they were embarrassed in Game 2 by a 7-4 score in front of their home fans. Then they had to go out west to Phoenix for Games 3 and 4.

Game 3 started perfectly for the Wings, as they scored two first-period goals. But that lead evaporated in the third period, as the Coyotes scored three unanswered goals and won the game. In the first series, the Wings found themselves down two games to one. They desperately needed a win in Game 4 to keep the series close.

Thankfully for them, they delivered. They won in Games 4 and 5 by two-goal margins before a decisive victory in Game 6, which ended in a 5-2 score.

The Red Wings ultimately dispatched the Coyotes in six games, notching two road victories in the process. They were one step closer to a victorious season they could deliver to Vladimir and Sergei.

In the second round, the Wings faced the St. Louis Blues, a familiar enemy over the past few years. The Blues must have done their homework because they went into Detroit in Game 1 and beat the Wings 4-2. Detroit responded, though, and won by a wide margin, 6-1, in Game 2. Back in St. Louis for Game 3, the teams were tied after regulation and remained tied at the end of the first overtime. In the second overtime, former Blues player Brendan Shanahan scored for the Red Wings to win the game. The Wings would win Games 4 and 6 from there to advance to the next round.

The Western Conference Finals featured the two best teams from the conference based on regular season records, the Dallas Stars and Detroit Red Wings.

Unlike the other series so far in the playoffs, the Red Wings began on the road, but they managed to win Game 1 by a score of 2-0. They lost Game 2 but managed to win Games 3 and 4 at home to have a chance to advance to Game 5.

The Red Wings nearly won Game 5, but they lost in overtime when their goaltender, Chris Osgood, unintentionally allowed a goal on a slap shot from center ice. What was even worse about that goal is that the original shot would have missed the net. But when Osgood reached out his stick to deflect the shot away, he mistimed it, and the puck deflected off the inside of his stick and went into the net behind him, sending the Dallas fans into a wild frenzy of cheers.

For a moment, Red Wings fans wondered if the hockey gods would not deem their team worthy of another championship, especially after how long they had waited for the previous victory. Thankfully, they didn't have to wonder much more, as the Red Wings won Game 6 to win the series and advance to the Stanley Cup Final. Chris Osgood made up for the mistake in Game 5 by stopping all 26 shots he faced.

The Detroit Red Wings, after a full year of playing without one of their core defensemen, had returned to the Final. The hockey world watched in awe as the team played inspired hockey all season, dedicating their performance to their fallen teammates. And now, the Stanley Cup was four wins away. The only team left with a chance to stop them was the Washington Capitals.

Thankfully, the Red Wings were up to the task, thanks in part to Konstantinov being present at each of the games. In fact, during stoppages in each game, he would be displayed on the video boards to all of the fans. This was done for the games in Detroit and Washington, but the results were the same. The fans of both teams stood and applauded the injured player.

The Red Wings needed a comeback and a goal in overtime to win in Game 2, but just like the previous year with the Philadelphia Flyers, Detroit was able to win the Stanley

Cup in four straight games to capture the title for a second year in a row. As the celebration on the ice took place, Konstantinov was brought down to ice level in his wheelchair to take part in the celebration with the team.

Now, when a team is awarded the Stanley Cup, it is brought out on the ice and presented to the captain of the team. Traditionally, the captain is the first player to raise the trophy over his head to begin the celebrations, skating it around the ice for all of the arena to see but Steve Yzerman did not take a lap with the Stanley Cup this time. Instead, he raised it over his head for a brief few seconds before lowering it onto the lap of Vladimir Konstantinov. The team cheered, and when they gathered together for a group photo, Vladimir was at the center of the picture, a peace sign in the air, a cigar in his mouth, and a smile on his face. The team had won the Stanley Cup for him.

Today, Vladimir Konstantinov still lives in the state of Michigan, as he receives continued medical care in the Detroit area. He is often invited to Red Wings special events and ceremonies as fans love to continue celebrating championships of the past, and he seems happy to be part of the community that has supported him through all of these years.

The 1997-1998 Detroit Red Wings will go down in history as one of the most inspirational stories of overcoming loss and finding the courage to succeed in the face of adversity. Although their first Stanley Cup victory in 42 years was cut short by the tragic limousine accident, their tenacity in capturing another championship likely made that second Stanley Cup even better.

Loss and suffering can sometimes be irreversible. However, that does not mean the end. Sometimes, a loss can be used to motivate and inspire, despite the pain that comes along with it. The loss can show you that life is short and fragile, and you might as well leave every ounce of effort on the ice when you get the chance. Remember this Red Wings team when you need a boost of inspiration in the face of loss.

STORY 9:

WILLIE O'REE BREAKS HOCKEY'S COLOR BARRIER

In the short history of the United States, one of the biggest issues that the country had to overcome was the institution of slavery. Even though slavery was abolished, there have been lingering issues with treating black people equally. Because of those lingering issues and troubling beliefs among some of the country's population, one of the key indicators of progress forward has been when black individuals make their way into areas of American culture, sports, and politics.

For example, the United States elected its first black president in 2008. This was a big step for the country. But sports have also been a substantial indicator of shifts in American culture. Many have heard of Jackie Robinson, the first black professional baseball player. He was an icon and inspiration to many people in the country and around the world. Hockey has a similar representation in its history.

Willie O'Ree was born in New Brunswick, Canada, in 1935. He grew up playing hockey in Canada, making it up to the Quebec Aces in the minor leagues. Willie O'Ree had a secret, though. During his time playing amateur hockey, O'Ree suffered a significant injury. Remember, players did not wear face protection at this point in hockey history. O'Ree, also not wearing a helmet, was hit in his right eye by a puck. Doctors tended to him, but O'Ree was able to hide the fact that he could no longer see out of his right eye. It's unclear how he was able to keep this a secret since eye doctors typically test each eye's vision separately, but O'Ree found a way. It was a good thing he did, too, because he wouldn't have been eligible to play in the NHL if the league had known about his injury.

However, during his second year with the Aces team, O'Ree was called up to the NHL ranks by the Boston Bruins, who needed to replace a player who was out with an illness. As the league didn't know about his injury, Willie O'Ree became the first black player in the NHL on January 18, 1958, when the Boston Bruins faced off against the Montreal Canadiens. O'Ree only played in one more game during that first season, and he would not return to the Bruins for two more years.

In the 1960-1961 season, Willie was called up for a much longer stint in the league. Again, with the Boston Bruins, O'Ree played 43 games out of the team's 70 regular season games. He managed to score four goals and record ten assists, for a total of 14 points. Four goals might not seem like a lot, but two of them were game-winners, which is pretty important during the course of a season.

While a half-season with below-average stats might not seem like a big deal in the world of hockey, there were a few incidents during the season that should be addressed if you want to understand O'Ree's full journey.

During one game in particular, when the Bruins were visiting the Chicago Blackhawks, a dangerous fight took place, and it would be a wake-up call to the NHL that things needed to change sooner rather than later.

Eric Nesterenko of the Blackhawks used the butt-end of his stick to hit O'Ree in the face, knocking out O'Ree's two front teeth, as well as breaking his nose in the attack. It was uncalled for. O'Ree had done nothing to deserve such a vicious attack; all he did was exist with a different skin color than the rest of the league.

O'Ree's response was to fight back, naturally, and he did so by hitting Nesterenko over the head with his stick. Now, in today's hockey, a player would be suspended, perhaps even banned from the league permanently. It's a wild scene to picture, considering the state of hockey today. But, O'Ree was not suspended, and he continued to play in that game.

Besides the physical altercation that night, there were allegations that the Blackhawks team and fans were calling

O'Ree racial slurs during the game. Likely, they were doing it throughout the game. However, it surely increased after what they had seen him do to Nesterenko. A butt-end attack is harder to see from the crowd than an overhead chop with the stick.

With all of this happening in the arena, O'Ree considered himself lucky to escape the arena alive that night. A scary world to live in, indeed, to fear for your own life in a room full of people you believe are out to get you. If you have not experienced this kind of hatred and fear for your own life, it could be a difficult emotion to understand. Thousands of people were enraged and wanted to attack O'Ree that night, but he did not let their hatred stop him from playing the game he loved. O'Ree likely experienced similar situations in most other places where his team played, although he did note that American fans were much more racist than Canadian fans.

Although Willie O'Ree never made it back to the highest level of professional hockey in North America, he did experience some significant success in the Western Hockey League with the Los Angeles Blades and the San Diego Gulls. He had three seasons where he scored more than a point per game, and he captured two scoring titles during his time in the league.

O'Ree played in various minor leagues until the age of 43 when he retired from the game. While he did not play the majority of his career in the NHL, his impact on the game has been enormous.

It's one thing to be the first black player to enter the NHL, but it's another thing to dedicate the rest of your working life to being an ambassador for the game. That is exactly what Willie O'Ree did. Think about a time when you accomplished something great. Did you pat yourself on the back and take it easy for a while? Maybe you did. It's not what Willie O'Ree did, though, because he was inspired to keep making a difference for other players, black and white, young and old.

But it would be quite a while before another black player made it to the NHL. Mike Marson was drafted in 1974 by the Washington Capitals, making him the next Black player to make it into the lineup of an NHL team.

Because of O'Ree's experiences with racism in the league, including that terrible incident in Chicago, the NHL took action and now requires players to undergo preseason diversity training every year. Furthermore, the league has created rules to eliminate racist language and verbal abuse from the game, punishable through both suspensions and fines. Sometimes punishments have to be used to help any stubborn players learn that their old behaviors are no longer acceptable. Maybe they become inspired to change so they don't miss a game or lose some of their money.

Willie O'Ree was also honored by several different organizations at many different levels, and some of them should be highlighted here. The New Brunswick Sports Hall of Fame inducted him into their ranks in 1984, an honor for anyone who hails from that province of Canada. But that was just the beginning of the accolades he would collect.

In 1998, Willie O'Ree was named the NHL's Diversity Ambassador, and he began spending much of his time traveling around the continent, promoting the game to schools and community programs. He also delivered messages that focused on the ideas of inclusion, confidence, and dedication as character traits on and off the ice. Part of his work with the NHL was also coupled with the NHL/USA Hockey Diversity Task Force, where he served as the director of youth development.

Through that non-profit program, O'Ree helped minority kids by encouraging them to learn and play the sport of hockey.

In 2008, O'Ree was honored by the Boston Bruins on the 50th anniversary of his first game in the league. He was also honored with a special exhibit focused on his career, which was displayed in the Sports Museum of New England. The government of Canada also awarded him the Order of Canada, which is bestowed upon civilians in the country that denotes honor, similar to military honor awards.

O'Ree's impact has been evident in the NHL, besides the rules made to remove racism from the game. NHL player Joel Ward, who played in over 12 seasons in the NHL for the San Jose Sharks, Washington Capitals, Nashville Predators, and Minnesota Wild, specifically cites Willie O'Ree as his inspiration to play hockey.

Imagine someone saying those words about you: "I made the decision to do what I'm doing today because I was inspired by you and the difference you made in this world."

Imagine how good it would feel to hear those words.

More importantly, consider what you might need to do if you want someone to say that to you one day. What better inspiration could there be?

Willie O'Ree broke the color barrier in the NHL. Until he had entered the league, every NHL player had been white. He might not have had any ethnically similar heroes in the NHL to look up to, but sometimes, great people don't need an example to follow. O'Ree decided for himself that he was going to do his best to become an NHL player. Because of his courage in the face of hatred, he has become the beacon for all young hockey players, demonstrating that anything is possible. There are plenty of sources of inspiration in his story, but it's up to you to decide which one is going to push you to greatness.

STORY 10:

AN EMOTIONAL SHUTOUT FROM CRAIG ANDERSON

Sometimes, an individual can be emotionally strong when it comes to issues going on inside themselves. When a person is diagnosed with cancer, they can often put on a brave face and remain tough for their family. In fact, some might say it is easier than the alternative. Well, in this story, Craig Anderson, an NHL goaltender, did not have the luxury of being able to keep his emotions inside to protect those around him, because he was not the subject of the tragedy.

Before we jump into the meat of the story, let's take a quick look at who Craig Anderson is as a hockey player.

Anderson grew up playing hockey in the United States, and since he lived in the Chicago area, many of the teams he played for as a child were from that same area. He was a member of the Chicago Freeze, a junior team that participated in the Quebec International Pee-Wee Hockey Tournaments in 1994 and 1995. These tournaments were popular for budding hockey talents to become well-known names around the hockey world at a young age.

As he got older, he chose to play in the Ontario Hockey League, where he suited up for the Guelph Storm. After one season with the Storm, Anderson was drafted with the 77th overall pick in the 1999 NHL draft by the Calgary Flames.

He would go on to play another season and a half in Guelph before his rights were acquired by the Chicago Blackhawks. At that point, he spent parts of three seasons playing for the Norfolk Admirals and the Blackhawks.

He was then acquired by the Rochester Americans, who are affiliated with the Buffalo Sabres. He spent most of the 2006-2007 season there, but also played five games with the Florida Panthers. From there, he would never go back down to the AHL.

For six years, Anderson had bounced between leagues, fighting for a chance to be called up by an NHL team. Finally, he had made his mark. He served as the second-string goalie in Florida for two more seasons, posting spectacular save percentages for each of those campaigns. Then, in 2009, he earned a starting job with a new team, the Colorado Avalanche.

His first year in Colorado featured a slightly above-average performance, but he only played 33 games in his second season with the team before he was traded to Ottawa. From 2010 to 2020, Anderson would play with the Senators, again posting great save percentage numbers throughout his time with the team.

During these ten years, Anderson came up against a significant emotional obstacle. In October 2016, his wife, Nicholle, went to the doctor for what she thought was a sinus infection. Unfortunately, after a series of tests, she was diagnosed with nasopharyngeal carcinoma, a rare cancer that affects the nose and throat.

Anderson's perfect life with his family and career came to a screeching halt as they grappled with the implications. He took a week off from traveling and playing with the team to be home with his wife, but once arrangements were made for further appointments and treatments, she encouraged him to return to the ice. That next game was against the Edmonton Oilers, in Edmonton. Going into the game, Edmonton was among the league leaders in goals, so it was going to be a difficult contest for any goaltender, especially with Anderson struggling with his wife's diagnosis. Even worse, Edmonton was on a hot streak, as they were coming into the game with a five-game winning streak in tow.

Put yourself in that situation. How could he compete when his wife, the woman he loves, was given a dangerous, possibly life-threatening diagnosis just a week ago? The pressure in his mind must have been enormous. But what happened in the game that night was something that no one could have predicted.

Through the first period, the game was scoreless. In the second period, the Senators got on the board, and Anderson managed to keep the likes of Connor McDavid and Jordan Eberle off the scoreboard. Ottawa took a 1-0 lead into the third. In the final 20 minutes, with a one-goal lead, the Senators were able to hold off a relentless attack from the Oilers, especially when the home team pulled in Cam Talbot for an extra attacker. When Bobby Ryan scored an empty net goal with 33 seconds left, Anderson pumped his arm and dropped to his knees in celebration.

After 60 minutes of tough, close-checking hockey, Craig Anderson made 37 saves and earned a shutout. Usually, when a team earns a shutout, there's a lot of celebrating. There's a team cheering and shouting for their goaltender. But that's not what the Ottawa Senators did for Craig Anderson.

They skated to his crease and hugged him. One at a time, they embraced the goaltender and shared a few words. They knew that the situation with his wife was weighing heavily on him.

When the three stars of the game were announced after the game and Craig Anderson was announced as the first star, he slowly took one circle around the neutral zone near his bench, holding his stick aloft to the fans applauding his effort, as tears ran down his face under the mask. Cam Talbot, the Edmonton Oilers goaltender that had just been beaten by Anderson's Ottawa Senators, was the only Oilers player who remained on his bench to applaud for Anderson during his curtain call. From one goaltender to another, Talbot understood the pressure that Anderson must have experienced during that game.

Any goalie can tell you that the pressure to play between the pipes is great. However, that pressure grows when a goaltender is working on a shutout. In the last few minutes of any game with a shutout on the line, nerves can play a big factor. Anderson must have felt some form of those nerves plus the anxiety of his family situation.

Further, every player in the league knew what Anderson was going through, and they all wanted him to know that they respected the performance he had just put on for that game.

While his wife underwent treatment for her condition, Anderson continued the season with the Senators. The team finished as the second seed in the Atlantic Division, and Anderson helped the team defeat the Boston Bruins and New York Rangers in six games each to reach the Eastern Conference Finals. Unfortunately, the team's run ended there when they lost to the eventual Stanley Cup Champion Pittsburgh Penguins in seven games.

The good news, though, is that Anderson's wife called him on the morning of that deciding Game 7 to let him know that she was officially cancer free. He didn't get a chance to go to the Stanley Cup Final, but he had the better prize of knowing that his wife was going to be okay.

At the end of the season, Craig Anderson was awarded the Bill Masterson Memorial Trophy for his perseverance regarding the situation with his wife. While he did not have to go through the cancer treatment, the emotional toll of the scenario was undoubtedly a significant stress on his life.

Craig Anderson's story shows that the people around you are important to your success. No man is an island, as the saying goes. But Anderson demonstrated his ability to maintain composure in his position as a goaltender, even when there was uncertainty regarding his wife's physical health. This is especially difficult considering how much focus is required for goalies to be successful. Unlike other players, they do not get to sit down at the bench every couple of minutes to gather themselves. They have to be paying attention for every second of a 60-minute game. Having to do that while your wife is struggling with a cancer diagnosis is extraordinary.

Be strong for those around you when you're needed, and you can be a source of inspiration for them and those around you.

STORY 11:

JIM KYTE DIDN'T LET DEAFNESS STOP HIM

If you've ever been to a professional hockey game, you know that the arena can get very loud. The music blasts out of the speakers, the fans clap and cheer, and the players call out to each other for the puck.

Now, imagine walking into that same arena for the hockey game and hearing nothing. You see people opening their mouths or clapping their hands, but you don't hear anything. You see players calling to each other for the puck and communicating plays with their mouths moving, but none of the sounds reaches your ears.

This is the experience that Jim Kyte had as a hockey player growing up in Canada.

But he also learned that blazing a new path meant providing opportunities to others. He unlocked a door that had been closed to players with disabilities for a long time. When he stepped through that door to his opportunity, he didn't turn around and slam the door shut behind him. Instead, he kept the door open and offered a helping hand to anyone else seeking to follow in his footsteps. Inspiration in leadership - but let's see how it happened.

Kyte was destined to be an athlete, it seemed since his father was John Kyte, who was named the Athlete-of-the-

Half-Century by St. Francis Xavier University in Nova Scotia, Canada. But he did not pick the same sport as his sibling, Aynslee, who was a member of the Canadian track team. Instead, he chose to play hockey, despite not being able to hear. It must have been a dangerous sport to learn since hockey requires knowing where everyone else on the ice is going.

Hockey players depend on their hearing to know if an opponent is skating close by, if a player is calling their name, or tapping their stick on the ice, which is a common communication method when a player wants the puck passed their way. Kyte was going to give it a shot, though, because he loved the game.

Before he became the first legally deaf NHL player, Kyte started with junior hockey in Canada. His first Ontario Hockey League season was with the Cornwall Royals in 1981, where he tallied 21 points in 52 games as a strong defenseman.

While his team lost in the playoffs, Kyte had impressed NHL scouts in his single season with the Royals of the OHL. He was drafted in the first round of the 1982 draft with the 12th overall pick by the Winnipeg Jets. That's an impressive feat in itself! In fact, there were 252 players selected in the 1982 draft, so for Kyte to be selected at number 12 is quite the honor.

Jim Kyte spent the next season with Cornwall, but he did play in two games for the Jets in that initial season. After that, Kyte would join the Jets as a full-time defenseman, playing in 58 games in the 1983-84 season. He would go on to play five more seasons with the Jets before being acquired by the Pittsburgh Penguins.

After the 1989-90 season, Kyte would begin splitting time between the NHL, IHL, and AHL with various teams, including the San Jose Sharks, Calgary Flames, and Ottawa Senators. In total, Kyte would end his hockey career in 1996-1997 with the Kansas City Blades of the IHL. In total, Kyte played 598 NHL regular season games, scoring 17 goals, 49 assists, and tallying 1,342 penalty minutes. He also played in 42 playoff games, where he notched six assists and 94 penalty minutes.

After his hockey career came to an end due to an injury suffered in a car accident, Kyte began looking for ways to make a positive impact on those around him as he recovered from his injury.

He co-founded the Canadian Hearing Impaired Hockey Association, giving hearing-impaired players a safe place to play the game. He also operated the Jim Kyte Hockey School for the Hearing Impaired for nearly a decade. He even had it operating in multiple cities across Canada.

What an impact that must have had on those individuals who want to play hockey but find it difficult, or impossible, because of their disability. Jim Kyte wasn't just inspiring them with his play on the ice. He went out of his way to clear hurdles for those individuals, to give them a push forward with their dreams.

He has spent much of his time with Algonquin College in Ottawa, where he created a Sports Business Management postgraduate program in 2002. In 2007, he was selected as the Academic Chair of the Marketing and Management Studies Department, which is part of the Algonquin College School of Business. During his time working at Algonquin, he worked toward and earned a master's degree in business administration from Royal Roads University. Two years later, he became the Dean of the School of Hospitality and Tourism at Algonquin College.

That's quite an impact to have on a school, bringing a full program to a college and then continuing to work toward the school's improvement, assisting the students in their push toward a degree.

In 2018, because of his trailblazing play in the NHL as the only deaf player ever, and his work across the country that has helped so many individuals on the ice and off, Jim Kyte was inducted into the Canadian Disability Hall of Fame. In the same year, he was also inducted into the Ottawa Sports Hall of Fame.

Despite a disability that many would find insurmountable, Jim Kyte pushed forward and created a path for himself. He was not equal to his peers because his hearing did not work. Jim Kyte did not complain about whether or not it was fair that he could not hear. He did not sit back and think that it was a hopeless situation. He definitely did not give up on his dream because of his disability. He put his head down and did the work to get to the NHL.

Then, when that work was done, he turned around and helped those with similar disabilities to walk a similar path, one that he had created for them. He sought out ways to give them the help they needed to be successful. He didn't tell them to just work hard as he had done. He didn't shrug and tell them they should figure it out on their own because he did. He helped. He inspired.

STORY 12:

BOBBY BAUN IGNORES A BROKEN LEG

When people think about hockey players, one of the first qualities that comes to their mind is toughness. Oftentimes, people will picture a guy with a few missing teeth in the front of his mouth, sometimes lost from the game that is still taking place, and the player only missed one shift so the dentist could get the bleeding to stop.

Well, every once in a while, a story of playing tough goes above and beyond comparison. This story isn't about teeth, stitches, or taped fingers. This story focuses on Bobby Baun, his unlikely contribution, and what the x-rays had to say after the series.

Very quickly, let's take a look at Bobby Baun's career stats, which may help you understand how much of a defensive asset he was. Baun played in a total of 964 NHL regular season games. He scored 37 goals, 187 assists, and 1491 penalty minutes. Just to clarify, Bobby Baun averaged a goal once every 33 games in the regular season. In the playoffs, his goal-scoring rate was nearly identical. Baun played in 96 playoff games, and he scored three goals. For a player who spent 17 seasons in the NHL, it's quite clear that his value came from his defensive play, or else, why would he have stuck around for so long?

With that background established, let's take a look at the moment when Bobby Baun found a way to inspire his team in a moment when they needed help.

The year is 1964, and it is Game 6 of the Finals. The Toronto Maple Leafs, who have won the past two Stanley Cups at this point, need a victory to force a Game 7 against the Detroit Red Wings. They are down 3-2 in the series, and they need someone to step up and help their team even the series if they want a chance to raise the trophy for a third time in a row.

The Red Wings are pressing in the third period to score a goal in a tied game, hoping to win the series immediately and win the Stanley Cup for themselves. As the Wings are looking for a way to score, they get a wide-open slap shot. Skating into the path of the shot for the block is sturdy defenseman Bobby Baun, who, again, is known for his excellent defensive play. The shot bounces heavily off his ankle, and Baun collapses to the ice in pain. He's able to continue for two more shifts in the third period until, during a defensive zone faceoff against Gordie Howe, he hears a popping sound from his ankle, and then he's completely unable to get up.

With no ability to put any weight on his leg, Baun is ultimately helped onto a stretcher, and his teammates and fans feared the worst. They might make it to overtime in this game, but their defense would be significantly weaker if Bobby Baun was unable to continue in overtime or Game 7.

They were wrong on more than one count, it would seem.

After Baun was removed from the ice and taken to the medical area in the arena, the Maple Leafs were able to escape the third period with the game still tied, meaning that overtime would be coming up soon.

Bobby Baun heard the news, and he knew he had to be on the ice to help his team. The doctors in the medical area had suspicious motives, though. One of them was the team's doctor, Dr. Jim Murray, and the other was an orthopedic surgeon from Chicago, Dr. Bill Stromberg. You would think that one of these doctors would understand the danger behind the injury and prevent Baun from going back out on the ice, but, even though Stromberg was from Chicago, he was a Leafs fan. And because of his fandom and desire for them to win, it was his "professional" opinion that Baun couldn't hurt his ankle any more than it already was. He suggested that the ankle be taped and frozen so he could return to the game.

Do you know what you don't have to pay attention to if your foot is frozen and taped so tightly that extra blood can't flow to it?

Your foot! Because you won't be able to feel it when it is frozen. The tape will prevent swelling and inflammation from taking hold, which will send even more pain signals throughout your body. All of the nerve endings will be useless, as they won't be able to send any signals to your brain. Any pain that Baun was experiencing from the blocked shot was delayed or completely blocked by the freezing of his foot, which allowed him the strength to lace up the skates once more and return to the ice for overtime.

He wanted to help his team with the must-win situation in overtime. If they did not score first, if the Red Wings managed to score a goal on the Maple Leafs, their season was over. What happened next was enough to inspire his entire team for more than one game.

So, after freezing and taping his ankle, he returned to the bench, which by itself is miraculous. It's very likely that when Baun's teammates saw him return to the game, they were motivated and inspired by his toughness. They would have likely thought, "If Bobby Baun is willing to return to the ice with only one good foot, maybe some broken bones, then I can skate harder and give more to the cause, too."

Has anyone in your life ever inspired you with their gutsy effort? If they have, then you know the feeling. It's strange to be on the other side of things, though. Bobby Baun wasn't doing it to inspire his team; he was doing it for the love of the game and the emblem on his jersey.

On the second shift of overtime, about one minute into the frame, Baun returned to the ice. He could skate, for the most part. The puck was in the offensive zone, and he was manning the blue line when the puck came his way. He let a weak shot go, perhaps because his balance was thrown off by the pain in his ankle. But magically, the puck seemed to have deflected off Bill Gadsby, one of the Red Wings' defensemen, and it found its way behind Red Wings goaltender Terry Sawchuk and into the net.

The Maple Leafs had won Game 6 on a goal from Bobby Baun, who could barely skate and rarely scored goals! The team was inspired by Baun's gutsy performance. In fact, they would be even more inspired when Baun played in

Game 7, refusing to get an x-ray to find out how bad the injury really was.

The team doctor, Dr. Murray, thought that Baun most likely had a hairline fracture in his fibula, but he couldn't convince Baun to sit out that final game. Instead, Baun insisted that his foot be frozen and taped again. He likely had this done between each period of that Game 7, as well.

Pushed on by the bravery of their teammate, the Leafs went on to win Game 7 by an impressive 4-0 score. They captured their third Stanley Cup in a row, and the celebrations around the city were massive.

Surely, Bobby Baun got an x-ray after Game 7, right? It would make sense since he did not have to play any more games. He could just take his time getting to the doctor and figuring out a recovery plan.

Well, no.

Reports are conflicting, but some stories claim that Baun was prepared to take part in the celebratory parade through the city, but he slipped and fell as he was getting into the convertible that was going to chauffeur him down the streets among the thousands and thousands of fans ready to celebrate with him. He didn't get a chance to be recognized by the city's mayor, which is sad, but he did finally get the medical attention he sorely needed.

Some even speculate that the fracture in his leg didn't happen until that fall before the parade, but it is impossible to say.

Now, this should not inspire you to ignore your injuries and continue to blindly push forward to victory. You should always listen to the advice of a medical professional when there is doubt about your physical health. However, there is an inspiration to be found in the grit of Bobby Baun. Hockey players have to be tough, and Baun's toughness is a prime example of how tough a hockey player can be, albeit to the extreme.

There is also inspiration in the idea of pushing your body to the limit in pursuit of a goal. In the heat of competition, gaining an edge over your opponent often requires pushing yourself harder than you are willing to push yourself. This applies to your on-ice endeavors, and the training you do off the ice. Whoever is willing to push more, train harder, and dedicate more of themselves to the cause is likely to be the one who is victorious at the end of the game.

Bobby Baun exemplified that toughness, tenacity, and willingness to push harder than his opponent, and he did it all for the love of the game.

CONCLUSION

Throughout all of these stories, many themes emerged. The first, the importance of which any young player should notice and recognize, is that making it up the ranks in the world of professional sports is a long grind. It's a difficult journey to find a spot in the strongest league in the world, and all of the players featured in these stories put in the work. It's inspiring to see how hard these players had to toil, on the ice and off, to develop the skills, physical strength, and mental endurance, to find their way through.

Second, it's crucial to remember that everyone involved in the game is a person, a human, just like you. Even though sports bring out the competitive spirit in everyone, and there is a desire to defeat your opponents, do not lose sight of the fact that, when the game is over, the opponents in the other handshake line are just people. They have loved ones. With that in mind, an air of respect for your opponents should be present in every moment, no matter how intense the battle on the ice becomes.

Finally, the goal of this book was to illustrate that people are capable of persevering through all kinds of trauma, pain, and trouble. Every individual in this book was up against a situation that tested their emotional and mental strength, but not always were they tested in the physical sense. This is an important point because you as the reader might think, "I'll never be as strong as these professional hockey players, so what's the point?" Well, these players and teams went through the typical physical stresses of the game, but that is not what made their stories special. Instead, the real inspiration in these stories comes from their choices, decisions, and how they responded to emotional and mental strain. It all comes down to choices.

You have the opportunity to make the tough choice, no matter your physical build. You have the chance to show the mental toughness and perseverance that these players have shown. And, even better, you have their stories to fall back on when you need a dose of inspiration or motivation. They have paved the way for you; now it's up to you whether or not you'll choose to walk those same paths. It will be difficult, but it will be worthwhile.

Hockey players are some of the toughest athletes in the world. To be successful on the ice, hockey players have to have the agility and balance to move around the rink on their skates; they have to see and understand where the puck is going, where their teammates are moving, and where their opponents are attacking; they have to be strong enough to win battles along the boards, muscling their way to the puck; they have to be dexterous enough to put the puck exactly where they want it to go.

All of this has to happen at the same time for a hockey player to have success. None of this can be affected negatively by things happening off the ice. To see what these individuals have gone through, yet they still achieved success, well, that is a true inspiration.

Thank you for reading this book. We hope that you have found a source of inspiration that helps you take the next step forward in your endeavors, whatever they may be. If you are looking for more inspirational hockey stories, we would recommend looking at the list of Bill Masterson Memorial Trophy winners, as those individuals all overcame great odds.

Here are just a couple of quick examples of what you might find:

- Bobby Ryan overcame struggles with alcoholism and PTSD, and then sought to help others with similar issues.
- Devan Dubnyk was traded between five different teams in two years, then he helped the Minnesota Wild go from last place to the playoffs with a great 2014-15 season.
- Jose Theodore had his best season in nearly a decade after his son passed away from complications related to the child's premature birth.

Hockey is brimming with stories like these for you to discover. If you don't yet have a favorite team or favorite player, it's never too late to find one. Every player in the league has had to overcome difficulties to get to the highest level of play in the world. Let their hardship inspire you to push forward in your endeavors.

Happy reading!